MW01519435

Pescetarian Is Not A Religion.
a book of musings

04/09/13

To Sushmita,

With affection

[signature]

Pescetarian

Is Not A Religion.

a book of musings

Anu Mukund

Pescetarian Is Not A Religion.
a book of musings

Written by: Anu Mukund.
Published by: SHVG Enterprises, Fairport, NY, USA.

First Edition: 2013

ISBN 978-1-4675-6722-0

Design and Production Consultants:
Resource Communications Pvt. Ltd, Bangalore, India

Dedicated to
My father: Thank you for your guidance.
My mother: Thank you for your encouragement.

To The Reader ...

I began writing this book as a service to society, myself included. Throughout my life, I have driven over many peaks and many valleys. And I've learned along the way to wear a seatbelt. Although we all have different journeys in life, we all have very similar "epiphanies". The question is, though, when will we strike upon those realizations?

This book is not meant to preach any ideals or opinions of my own. Rather, I used it as a tool to help me to sift, organize, and unravel why things happen the way they do in life. I subscribe to the thought that we are never done learning, never done growing. I've had many questions along the way and I'm sure I'll have infinite more. But writing things down helps me absorb everything I experience in my environment. I know many others feel the way I do, and I thought, why not enjoy our findings together?

With that in mind, I have dedicated each chapter of this book, chronologically, to a specific question that came to my mind and has visited me many times thereafter. And after learning from guidance that has never led me wrong, I can now enjoy seeing things clearer, for what they really are.

I believe the excitement of knowing you are never done learning is something to be shared. I hope this humble offering to society sparks that same interest to learn and grow in others as it has in me.

Anu Mukund
Rochester, New York

Contents

Omega fail.

Ever have those moments where you look back at the past five minutes of your life and think, "Man, I really set myself up for that embarrassment."? Well, I've had a lot of those. But the best part about these incidents? They usually make for funny stories in retrospect. Here's one of my personal favorites...

It was my last year of college and, like many upperclassmen, I thought I pretty much ran the place. One of my reigning locations was the on-campus café and I visited it daily. Okay, who am I kidding, I went there at least four times a day. I used to work there after all and was seriously addicted to caffeine after four years of sleep deprivation. As I waltzed to the counter to place my afternoon order, I saw one of my former colleagues, and more importantly, one of my dear friends. We chatted for a few minutes at the counter, catching up on each other's lives, while I felt about twenty pairs of eyes glaring impatiently at the back of my head.

As we talked for a bit the topic of food came up. At this point, I don't really remember how it came up but I'm always hungry so it's not surprising that the conversation took a gourmet turn. Anyway, I think we ended up talking about sushi and, as a vegetarian, I mentioned how much I loved avocado in my sushi rolls. To which my friend responded *that since she's a pescetarian, it's one of the few things on campus that she can eat and still find delicious.*

And that's where I got this confused look on my face and asked ignorantly, "But, I thought you were Buddhist?" My friend stopped and stared for a few seconds, probably deciding how to answer. I honestly don't blame her; in hindsight, I don't know how I could have been that clueless. When she did answer, she cleared up my confusion by telling me that being pescetarian means being a vegetarian and throwing in some fish on your plate as well. After that we both laughed, me a little more due to my embarrassment at confusing fish for faith, and we went on with finally placing my afternoon regular.

So that's my story. And I thought it would make for a catchy title. I'd like to thank you for giving my book a chance. It's my first time trying it out as a writer, so please bear with me. Why did I write this book? What's it about? Well, turn the page and I think you'll find some answers.

Did I do that?

It's late afternoon on a Tuesday and you're in your second semester of college. You just came out of another midterm and the seasons are finally showing their first signs of change. Leaves are starting to sprout, birds are chirping, and it's finally warm enough for you to forget your heavy coat. You feel a sense of relief and freedom but it's quickly stomped out by the feeling of foreboding about that huge project due in your Thursday morning class. You tell yourself, "Ok, let's take a small break. Watch the latest episode of *How I Met Your Mother*, grab a good lunch, and then get back to work. You know if you don't start today, you'll be in huge trouble on Thursday morning. That individual project counts as half your grade."

After finishing a satisfying veggie wrap and iced vanilla latté to the comedy of Neil Patrick Harris, you say to yourself, "Ok, let's do this! A+ here we come! Who said keeping up with schoolwork in college was hard? This is a piece of cake." You pull out a bulky folder filled with various handouts and finally single out the guidelines to your upcoming project. You glance down at the bulleted section your professor has constructed that states the minimal amount needed for a passing grade, followed by the percentages allotted to each portion of the project grade. Taking a deep breath, you exhale as you think of how *imperative it is for you to have a stellar submission. Your past exam results in this class were not top notch and this is your last shot at pulling off a perfect grade in the class. At this moment, the familiar mental debate of whether curved classes are really a blessing or a curse visits you once again.*

Just as you're about to pick up that ridiculously large psycholinguistics book, your phone rings. It's a text message from your friend. A group of your friends are going to the park and getting ice cream after! As much as you crave to join them, you send them a crestfallen response, telling your friends you need to focus on your project. After seeing the little envelope emoticon on your phone fly off into the distance, you try to get your focus back to your task at hand. Just as you pick up a pen to attempt to jot down some brainstorm ideas, you hear your phone ring again. It's another text from your friend telling you how much fun it would be for all of you to enjoy the afternoon together.

You reconsider the proposal. It's the first time all your friends have been free in months and you do really love ice cream. Going to the park is exercise, right? Doesn't Dad always say you need to go out and get some fresh air before trying to concentrate on a huge assignment? Well he says something like that, and he's a professor, so it's valid, isn't it? Anyway, you have ALL of Wednesday to focus on your project. Get all of your energy out of the way today; that way all you'll want to do tomorrow is concentrate on your project. And maybe you can even start tonight after you get back!

Thinking you've got the perfect plan for the perfect grade, you go out with your friends. Hours later than you expected, you return to your room and think, "Wow! What an awesome day! The park was so beautiful and I haven't thrown around a Frisbee in forever! Sure, we took a bit longer than I thought we would, but spending time with friends and enjoying life is what matters right? I can't believe none of my friends have anything else to do for the rest of the week."

At that's when you remember with a wrenching feeling in your stomach, that you have 34 hours left to start and finish your project. But it's already 10:00 p.m., you're exhausted, and you need to rest to make the most of your time tomorrow. Let's sleep and start fresh tomorrow.

You wake up ready to go! Showered, fed, and pumped to rock this project. But as you sit with your assignment, coffee in hand, you realize that this project requires a lot more preparation than you expected. It sounded so easy when the professor explained it. And just like that, your panic mode ensues and you just wish you had more time. You could do such a solid job if you just had one more day. "Why did I go out yesterday? Sure, it was a lot of fun but I could have gone out with them when I was honestly free. My friends aren't going anywhere. It's ok that they went out; they're actually free! Oh man, I hope I can finish this and submit something decent in time…"

There are times in every person's life when they look back at certain moments and think, "Why did I do that?" "Did I really say that?" Looking at your life at present day you wonder, "I'd never do that now, so why'd I do it then?" Many times, we convince ourselves that what we are doing is acceptable. And perhaps what we've convinced ourselves isn't necessarily wrong, but it's just not beneficial at that point in time. As conscientious people, we strive to do things that are "correct" and many times, that "correctness" is shaped by society. Humans are social beings by nature and at a subconscious level, of course, we all want to be liked and accepted by those around us.

And maybe this starts when we are very small. As children, our world revolves around our parents and their love. We want to be celebrated by them and we vie for their attention through a little something called the reward/punishment system. To please our parents and be rewarded by praise and treats is a collective childhood dream. Who doesn't want to be loved and pampered by their parents? A stuffed animal here, a Rice Krispie treat there. When we were children, our brains were not fully developed and we didn't have the analytical tools to define what is right and wrong. And so acceptance conditioning begins at this tender age.

After a few years, when we are around five years old and begin school for the first time, we seek the acceptance of our teachers as well as our parents. A gold star on our Clean-Up Chart is all we strive for, so that we can be the teacher's pet and tell our parents the good news when they pick us up. We assume that our teachers and parents are keeping our best interest in mind. And, although that might be part of their reasoning, there may be many facets to their behavior. If our teachers know that they could get a promotion if all their children are well behaved when the principal checks in on their class next week, our teachers would create twenty star charts to get that raise. That's not to say that our teachers don't care about us, but that they are also considering what is best for them.

Well, what about our friends? At this age, although companionship is nice, we don't really need it. To say we care about friendship outside of our family and teachers at this point would be a stretch. Since, children do not have the faculties to think deeply about right and wrong, good and bad, they are able to fight and make up within seconds: Your friend takes away the truck you were playing with. That's not fair! You hate your friend. Ten minutes later your friend comes back and offers you a car to play with the truck. You are best friends again! Life is great!

Fast forward some years more and we're in middle school, the land of awkwardness. And here's where it's mandatory that we fit in. If we don't, we're basically committing social suicide. Dramatic as it sounds, we've all felt that moment where we think if we are at least accepted by our peers, things will be ok. And that mindset travels with us to high school where we wish to be lauded by our classmates. We wear what we think is cool, use slang we know sounds stupid but, hey, it's what everyone else is saying, and we pray that by blending in with all our peers, we'll somehow stand out.

But herein lies our dilemma: we want to be accepted and coveted by all our social groups. And at those oh-so-awkward moments, sometimes these groups collide. Try as we might to avoid their interaction, it's bound to happen. We've either been that kid or seen our friends squirm in mortification when their mom talks to the coolest kid in our group of friends. *Why'd she have to choose him of all the kids in the group! Oh God, she's mentioning our band performance. No, Mom, he plays the drums! Not the saxophone! Kill me now.* And although you may be burning into oblivion from embarrassment, neither your friend nor your mother is aware of your meltdown. So why are you? Are you crazy? No. Maybe it's just that you know subconsciously that there's a difference in what is acceptable to your friends and to your family. And so you've tried your best to separate these groups completely so that you can reap the benefits from both groups. Think this is selfish? It's not, really. You're just trying your best to get the optimum rewards from all your social settings.

And now, years later, we are in college, working, or both, our rights of passage into adulthood. Finally those mental faculties are maturing℠ and we start considering

---

℠   For some, a bit sooner than others.

what we want from life. We are in constant limbo of achieving immediate rewards and long-term goals and this causes a complicated set of personal expectations. And we experience inner conflict when we notice that the demands of our social groups may interfere with our long-term goals. We make feeble attempts to think about our future goals, but our thoughts are immediately squashed when we assume that if we do not do what we think is accepted by our friends or acquaintances, we will be missing out on something. Our future plans are shoved to the side and we convince ourselves that what we are doing in the moment is just fine.

Cue our original story about our park and project debate. How could we have avoided this situation in the first place, instead of regretting our decision later? Obviously, we can't walk away from society completely. And sure, we've all made the mistake of assuming that if we do not join our pals on a certain occasion, we will be rejected as a result. But that's not necessarily true! How do we know that that's all it takes for a friendship to break? If we have the confidence to assert what we feel is best for ourselves, perhaps our friends will understand. But we've got to try to find out, right?﷽

﷽   If you think what this group is doing could wipe out your future in one fell swoop, it's definitely not worth it to be accepted by this group. Sure, we all need a group of friends, but you don't necessarily need this specific one, if they totally don't gel with what you think.

So we need to decide, how much are we willing to give up our plans for the long term to suit our nearsighted wants? Say our friends want to go out every night, not just the random Tuesday. We've got two options: the first is to avoid them completely if what they do totally contradicts what we think is alright. But if we do decide to change our group, we should make sure we have another group to fall into.

That choice is pretty extreme. Maybe what this group does is not so bad. In our situation, going to the park is not a terrible thing and going out for ice cream with friends is completely harmless. So let's keep our friends and look at our second option. Question: what is the minimum reward from this group that is acceptable to you and that will still allow you to be part of this group? Goofing off every afternoon may completely ruin your grades, but going out once or twice a week when you don't have assignments due the next day may give you enough rewards where you enjoy the company of your friends, feel part of the pack, and still manage to excel in schoolwork. If you have legitimate reasons why you cannot hang out with these people, and if they are sensible, they will understand. But we need to have the confidence in ourselves to define what is best for us.

We must always analyze the reward system in this broad sense. We'd only be lying to ourselves if we said we didn't need to. Now that we have the ability to analyze what we were conditioned to think or do by society at a young age, we must wonder whether what we were told was and is actually true. Regardless of whether our conclusions are accurate, it's worth considering. Are the thoughts we were told to support proven true through our own experiences? Obviously, there is no absolute right and wrong in life. Rather than making such ultimate dividers, observe that there is a relationship between every action and every thought, and they are followed by a consequence. And the best part about all of this? The silver lining is that perhaps today's long term reward was yesterday's future reward, and will be tomorrow's short term achievement.

Hey now, that's pretty awesome.

*T*aking a break from your daily study routine, you decide to watch a movie in the theater with your friends. You watch a late night screening of the latest Bond installment. To your surprise, it wasn't as riveting as its predecessors. As you and your friends exit the theater through the glass double doors, you open your mouth to voice your opinion. Just then one of your friends exclaims that the movie was the best Bond film yet! Your other friends agree with enthusiasm and you find yourself smiling and nodding in consensus, keeping your review in your head.

The next week, while walking to class, you bump into that acquaintance you've been meaning to get to know better. He asks you to coffee and you oblige, agreeing to meet up at the campus coffee shop after class. Ninety minutes later, as you look forward to your upcoming caffeinated conversation, you wonder what you will talk about. After getting your latté, you sit down across from your new friend; you suddenly think of the Bond movie you saw last weekend.

"Hey, did you see the latest Bond movie?"

"Yup, I did. How about you? What did you think of it?"

"Yeah, I went this past weekend. It was awesome. Seriously the best Bond film yet." As the words come out, you feel as if you are reciting your friend's script from Saturday.

"Oh…I actually didn't think it was that good. I was expecting a lot more, I guess. I think the previous Bond movies were much better."

And that's when you think to yourself, Wow! He thinks just like me! I assumed everyone loved the movie, but how can I go back and change my opinion now? And I said it with such conviction, too. Oh man, I should have just said what I actually thought.

Though we may be independent, confident creatures, there's always that little voice in us that keeps wondering, what do other people think of me? Do people think of me the way I'd like them to think of me? Am I fitting in with my surroundings? When you mull over those questions long enough, you'll come to find that it really comes down to two distinct reasons.

The first is that we look outside constantly and completely. I mean, even nature has created us to seek our information from the outside world. Our senses relay that exterior raw data to our mind and as we blend all that information into a grey muck, we forget that without seeking intellectual thought from ourselves, we'll only lead ourselves to conflicting conclusions.

Let's say you met a new classmate and from your first conversation, you guys seemed to really hit it off. Turns out two of your friends know this person too and you ask them what they think of that person. Friend 1 says the person is great and really nice. Friend 2 says the person is bizarre and not honest. Now these are two very conflicting reviews of the same person. So it'd only be natural to be left confused and wondering whether to continue getting to know your new friend or not. Instead of looking at your experience with the person, which is positive, you have concluded certain declarations based on no personal experience of your own.

And after a while of doing this, one fine day it dawns on each of us that others gather their impression of you in a similar way; by asking others what they think of you. And once that comprehension settles in, you will hope that you have laid the best basis for people to judge you by. The "right" things to eat, wear, listen to, all become of utmost importance and end up altering our behavior. Although our internal attitudes will continue to be the same, our outward appearances will morph in attempts to have people keep us in positive review.

But how do we really know if all that hard work will really pay off? If a person jokes in passing that we're stupid, do they actually assume we're stupid? Some may even go as far as asking them if they really think so. Even if the question's brushed off and the statement is passed off as a joke, what if it wasn't? How can we ever be sure? Let's take a step back and realize that it doesn't really matter what they think. The spoken opinions of people (us included) on a subject are constantly changing. And as much as we may strive to create the "perfect" impression of ourselves to the outside world, it will never transcend to every single person around us. As long as we know that we are who we are, what does it really matter what others think of us?≋ No matter what we do, people will think of us as they want to. And that's okay. As long as we have the self-confidence to know it's alright to be who we are.

Which leads us to the second reason why we worry so much about what others think of us: maybe we just don't know who we are yet. We don't know what our strengths are, what our weaknesses or our irritating habits are.

≋   Whether it's about a Bond movie, the menu at a local restaurant, or anything else, why think our opinion has no value? We don't bash others' thoughts so we shouldn't bash our own before they even come out of our mouths. And hey! Our anti-cookie cutter perspective makes for more interesting conversation, too! Work with it!

And it's hard for us to look at ourselves objectively, without any bias. It's always easier to point the finger at the other person, or the situation, instead of asking what may be wrong with us so that we can work to correct it.

But if we need to look at ourselves, it'd be pretty handy to have a mirror, or anything that can present a reflection of who we are. A fun house has many mirrors but none are an accurate representation of reality. We look to others to serve as our mirrors. But how do we know that it's an honest portrayal? How do we know the mirror is not flawed?

Need an example, you say? Of course, I'll oblige! It is difficult to be completely objective with your family. Parents could praise their kid with the honest belief that their child is doing something right. Or, parents could be praising their child in front of other parents to boast of their child's success so that they can know on the drive home that their kid is superlative. Many times parents justify what their kids are doing, even if they know it's not correct.

And being objective is much easier said than done. So where is that ultimate mirror? The answer to that question leads us to a solution for our two reasons of worry. Instead of looking at people's reaction to you, look at what comes your way. Keep doing what you think is right according to your personal set of beliefs, regardless of others' reaction. Immediately, your stress level of how you seem to others will deflate.

By continuing this lifestyle, you'll notice in the long run that whenever you are in need, help will always come and in large quantity at that. And it may not be from the people you would necessarily expect. But society is always observing what its citizens are doing. And if you keep chugging along, doing what is best for you, others will notice and those "unflawed mirrors" will come forward.

Keep in mind, what is right for one person may not necessarily be right for someone else. And that's okay. There is no absolute right and wrong, so why should we look to others for that confirmation? Sometimes, the mirrors we choose to look into are not the right ones for us. But wouldn't it be nice if the mirrors meant for us presented themselves to us on their own? If we have that self confidence in ourselves, our beliefs, and what is right and wrong *for us*, in due time, we will find that who we are is reflected in glimpses around us.

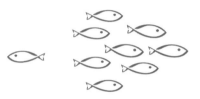

Never mind, you don't get it.

You wake up with a jolt and sit up straight in your bed. You look at your phone for the time: 4:30 a.m. Your half hour nap passed by you in a restless flash and you scramble to your desk, turn on the light, and, while staring at the results section of your English paper, desperately try to orient yourself with reality. "Okay, that paragraph seems alright. Three down, who knows how many more to go..."

Two hours later, you are feverishly completing the last paragraph of your conclusion. You glance nervously at your laptop's clock hoping it's only been a half hour since you woke up. It's 6:35 a.m. Crap. You have forty-five minutes to proofread, print, and trek the half-hour power walk over to the English department. It's just your luck that you have the toughest TA in all the sections and you know that if you're even one minute late, he'll take off 10 points on your paper.

As you burst into the computer room with two minutes to spare, you thrust your paper in the direction of your TA, and collapse at your table, attempting to collect yourself and whatever little oxygen you have left in your lungs. The worst is over, you think to yourself and, as the class begins, you feel a sense of pride that you completed your paper on time and, that too, with all the work required for an A.

The following week, as you stroll into class, you look forward to the ravishing A you expect to see on your graded paper. As your name is called, you swagger to the front of the room and thank your TA in a professional, I know I've got this, kind of way. As you look down at your paper you are appalled to see a B– blemishing your hard work. Confusion, anger, and disappointment come in one simultaneous blow and as you take your seat you feel that loathing sense of dejection.

Dejection turns to rebellion and you wait impatiently for your class to end so that you can blow off the rest of the day. You plan to meet your friend for lunch, and since he had the same TA last year, you feel it only fair to share your woes with him. Who better to understand your problem?

As you and your friend settle down with your trays at an open table, you start to tell him the saga that is your English paper. He nods thoughtfully and after you finish with all the right points of dramatics, you are shocked to see that your friend is not very fazed with the situation. He simply says, "That's too bad. I know, that TA is tough."

Tough? That TA was so unfair! He took off points for the most random reasons! The lack of emotion your friend expresses pulls you down further than before lunch and, although you enjoyed your time with your friend, you find yourself craving a session of self-pity and sleep. As you walk to your dorm room on that bright sunny day you call your

*dad and recount your story. To your dismay, your dad
listens to your whole story and though he gives you a pep
talk about how you'll get a better grade next time, you find
no satisfaction. Irritated with yourself and the day's events,
you crash onto your bed, waiting for sleep to commence.
Clamping your eyes shut, you think to yourself, why doesn't
anyone understand?*

We've all had that moment of self-pity where we crave for others' comfort. But no matter how much we get from others, it never seems to be enough. Why? Maybe it stems from two different possibilities: either others are not making enough effort to try to understand your situation, or perhaps the cause lies in the fact that we do not understand our own problems.

It's not that others cannot understand your problems; it could be that they are just not paying enough attention to the issue at hand. It's human nature to be involved in our own problems. We magnify our own concerns and downplay others'. It's not anyone's fault, really. But we're so used to focusing on our own problems and assume that if we were to go through another's problems, we'd be able to handle it easily and with more grace.

And when we feel down, we seek comfort from those around us. Like a blanket on a chilly night, we indulge in self-pity when things do not go our way. We look for warmth from our environment. Whether it's from a blanket or a fire in the hearth, it's not coming from us. It's a fact that, at this moment, we're not able to supply ourselves with the warmth, or better yet, the energy, to push through our concerns on our own. If we were full of energy, we wouldn't seek comfort from others, and we'd push through our problems without such severe levels of worry. I'm not saying we're designed to be completely energized at all points of time, nor am I endorsing year long subscriptions to 5-Hour Energy® drinks. It's perfectly normal to not be at our level best all the time. But we need to think of where our energy is being diverted and, when it is, how to get it back.

Regardless of the topic, no matter how much we try to find that sole source of comfort from others, we won't be satisfied. After that nap following the "English paper catastrophe", we probably would feel much better. Why? Because when we were slogging over that paper, our last concern was proper sleep. After getting some rest, we feel much better and realize that maybe the points our TA made on our paper make sense and we can use that to do better in the future. Dad was right, and there's no need to worry.

And that thought serves as a transition to the second possibility: that maybe the issue is that we do not understand our own problems. If we knew how to approach our own problems we would not look to others for understanding. Every person has a unique set of experiences. And if those around us have not had the same experiences, it may be impossible for them to even comprehend our situation.≋ But if another person does have knowledge of your experience, they will still never be able to *understand* you; but they can *empathize* with you.

But as the cliché saying goes, history repeats itself. And most of our experiences are similar and shared. After all, we are all exposed to the same world. What makes us unique is our personal reaction to the experience. And because our personal reactions to our experiences are unique, our outcome from the situations

---

≋   Of course, there could be cultural differences in context. If you wish to see a concert with your friends and don't have the money or your parents won't allow you to, your experience will be the same as when your mother was young and wasn't able to see a movie with her friends because she didn't have the money or her parents wouldn't let her go. The context is different; the feeling is the same.

will be unique as well. Not to mention our feelings will be very different based on our prior experiences.

So we need to clarify what we are looking for in others. We are not looking for understanding. We are looking for empathy. Deep down, maybe we know that no one else will ever be able to truly understand our experiences and us. And how can they? Words are a terrible medium to try to share an experience.※ Just like the saying goes, "words cannot describe..." we can never truly transfer our experiences to others, try as we might. And as much as our friends and family may try to empathize with us, after some time, they will tire of our problems and will lose interest. And that is when we feel that no one understands us.

Maybe we've subconsciously self-inflicted the idea that we are more special than those around us. From the time we are little, we are fed by society that we are each completely unique and incomparable. And perhaps in some ways we are, but to think our problems are greater than all those around us is an exaggeration. The metrics by which we measure our worth may be

---

※   Ever try to explain to someone close to you just how special or important something is to you? It could be a song or a movie or just a moment in time. But after you try your best to get your message across, you still wonder if they really got it? That's what I'm talking about here.

completely skewed from reality. People rate themselves on looks, wealth, social status, and the list goes on. Though we may not say it out loud, if we keep ourselves on a pedestal, can't our attitude be unwarranted?

So what's the solution to this predicament? If we ask ourselves who knows us better than anyone else, the answer is simple and clear: ourselves! Who could know you better than you? We never tell our every single thought or action to any one person, no matter how close they are to us. But we can't hide from ourselves. That being said, do we want to merely seek comfort or do we want to seek solutions to our problems? At the end of the day, our concerns belong to us and so we can only expect they will always be of priority to us. But that doesn't mean we should completely sign off on those around us. Others can always give us resources to deal with our issues, be it financial, emotional, or intellectual. Perhaps their own personal experiences allow them to relate to our own. We need to find a compromise between seeking encouragement and support from others and working on a solution ourselves.

Comfort, as lovely as it is, is always a temporary satisfaction. Comprehension of our concerns and solving our problems with our own solutions is the only way for personal growth. That security of knowledge from our experiences will only help us in the future and give us the energy inside to stay strong throughout our future endeavors.

You really mean that ●

*You look at your roster of the thirty-eight names assigned to
your floor. As it's your first year as Resident Assistant, you're
pretty impressed that, after only two weeks, you've been able
to match a face with almost all of your floor-mates. You've
tried to apply your summer RA training as best as you can,
hosted meetings for your residents to get to know each other,
and hope that you will be able to make your Hall Director
proud while still having a good rapport with your floor.*

*After arranging some things in your room you look out
your window to see the sun on its descent for the day. It's a
Friday afternoon in September, early enough in the semester
where midterms and final grades are more of urban legends
than reality. You notice many students outside playing
football, catching up with old friends, or just soaking up
some last minute rays of sun. You wish you could be out
with your friends too, but then remember you have your first
round of night duty.*

*Two knocks sound on the other side of your door and
you walk towards it to answer. As you open the door you
see a very familiar face with a big smile; it belongs to one
of your residents. Thanking you for a warm welcome to
college she offers you a cupcake she picked up at the campus
deli. You feel flattered by this first token of appreciation and
ask her what her plans are for the weekend. She replies by*

saying nothing special, really. Just that she and some other freshmen are planning on meeting up tonight. You wish her a good evening with a smile and shut the door thinking the semester's off to a great start.

Hours later, you find yourself in the RA Office on the first floor. You've had a pretty easy shift, needing to help just a few kids locked out of their rooms. You look at your half eaten cupcake, and as you reach for another bite, the office phone rings. You listen to the student on the other end asking for an RA to tell their neighbors to lower the music in their room. You ask for the room number and you notice the complaint is coming from your floor.

You climb up the stairs to your floor and reach the room that's booming with a loud consistent bass and a muffled choir of voices. You knock three times on the door and suddenly, the music is gone and the voices are silent. There's a pause and a quiet murmur on the other side and eventually the door opens. You are surprised to see the same girl who gave you a cupcake hours earlier looking back at you and then remember this is her room.

You politely ask them to keep the noise down and inform them this is the first warning and after that if there's another complaint they'll have to be written up. Your resident apologizes for the noise and promises to make sure there aren't any more problems. Feeling your job is done here, you walk back down to the office contentedly and settle down for the rest of your shift. Half an hour passes and two calls reach you, one after the other. Complaints lodged about the same room, once again. You didn't want it to get to this, but you pick up the forms required and march up to your floor. Again, you hear the loud booming of music and voices and knock on the door. Silence meets you as you see, this time, about twenty people crammed into the small room. You ask your two residents to fill out the forms and shut down the party.

As you leave the room, you wish there were some sort of good cop/bad cop scheme you could have used, with you being the good cop, of course. You don't like writing them up, but you didn't have a choice. As you leave the room, you look at your two residents with an encouraging smile, hoping they'll take it as a sign that there are no hard feelings from your side. You finish out your shift with no further problems and scramble into your bed at 2:00 a.m., thankful you can finally sleep.

The next day, you wake up late knowing you don't have duty today and rise out of bed with a smile. Grabbing your shower caddy from your closet, you slip on your flip-flops hoping a shower stall will be free. As you lock up your door

*you hear shuffling at the end of the hall and see the girl who
gave you the cupcake walking in your direction. You smile at
her and wish her a good morning. To your dismay, she does
not smile back and makes a minimal attempt to acknowledge
you, while still being civil. She passes by you and enters the
bathroom. You think back to the note that she had written
on top of the pastry yesterday that read, "To the best RA!"
Walking towards the bathroom you wonder, "Did she really
mean that?"*

Whether from ourselves or from society, we
have collected a number of assumptions about
the world and the people around us. One being that
the people we keep closest to us, our family, friends,
colleagues, have our best interests at heart. But what if
what they tell us is not necessarily always in our best
interest? When should we listen and when should we let
a comment just slide?

I sized this conundrum down to two key components:
by experience, how wise is this person and how does
this person react to a given situation? You can tell a lot

about a person by just observing them.﷽ Many times, those who openly advertise their experiences without any prompt aren't the ones who have the best advice to dish out. They might just like to hear the sound of their own voice. I don't mean to sound harsh, but the saying "actions speak louder than words" is really convenient to quote here.

Also, the metrics used in society previously to gauge wisdom have now become political. Not literally—that politicians are always the wisest of us all—but in a broad sense that society may not necessarily be projecting the wisest persons at the forefront of their genre. And by definition, a wise person would never go out of his or her way to seek recognition.﷽﷽

So instead of trying to track someone's history, let's look at someone's behavior that's demonstrated right before our eyes. Like I said before, there's a lot to be said

---

﷽ When we look back at our past, sometimes things get a little fuzzy and at times romanticized. So when we ask others about their experiences, we need to remember that sometimes facts may be a bit skewed. Not to say we need to always take what they say with a grain of salt, but it'd probably be best to see things from a third-person's point of view, without getting too attached to what they say.

﷽﷽ Take the Nobel Prize. With all due respect to all the scholars nominated for the award, how do you know the person who receives the award is the wisest of them all? Doesn't that depend on whom you're asking? The award committee will have its own agenda and will award someone based on their collective needs as well. So we can't go strictly by those metrics.

for a person's reaction to a situation. Wise people tend to be more at peace with themselves and that shines through in their actions. Wisdom is like a rock; it weighs you down and holds you and your emotions at practical levels. They still care about what's going on around them but they're able to take in what's going on around them, absorb that information, and come to a reasonable and warranted reaction.

Well doesn't that sound just peachy! And if wisdom was so simple to achieve wouldn't we all have it, all the time? But it's a lot easier said than done. This type of strength and durability takes time, concentration, and effort. So how can we differentiate a wise person from someone who is not? Well, going in the opposite direction on the wisdom spectrum, wouldn't it be a person who can get highly worked up or excited easily? Even the smallest of things, even if they know it is not a huge deal, will be made into one by their reaction.

All right, so now that we've defined the difference between the two, how do we know who to listen to? Look around us. Those people who are wisest will not be the first to open their Peanuts' Lucy-esque Nickel-For-Your-Thoughts Stand. They may warn a person but they will only advise when asked. Those who tell you something on their own may wish you the best, but they themselves may not know what is good for you. And based on what the other person is saying, is there something of you that they want?

So what, now we're supposed to live in fear that everyone is using us? Not at all! But why jump to extremes either way? Constant paranoia that others are out to get you is a terrible way to live a life. Let's just assume people are the best, but not put blind faith in them either. After all, we are all human and we all have our own specific flaws.

Okay, so it's not really a question of analysis; we don't have enough data to "analyze" anything. If we did, we wouldn't be asking these questions. So instead let's ask, how do we find truth in what we see around us? Here are three different routes.

The first is by experience. If someone tells you something to the contrary of what you've personally experienced, they may be wrong or perhaps your own conclusion is incorrect. If you are committed to your previous conclusion, be cautious if it's based on one experience. The more repeated experiences you have, the more faith you can put into your deduction. In reality, we'll never really know for sure, but there's a question of how much faith you are putting into this theory.

The second is by listening to what others have told you. We must see for how long certain truths have been held in place. It could be anything as simple as general advice, sound quotes, or just known observations. But if people, time and time again, have put their faith in something that has proven to be true, there must be something to that, right?

The third is by inference. This is separate from analysis. Analysis, like we said earlier, is when you use your intelligence to go through some data you have and eventually derive a conclusion. But inference is going from truth to truth and coming to conclusions based on those pre-existing truths. We are not starting from blind data, here.

So maybe it's not a question of using just one of these routes over the other. Maybe it's more about mixing them all and creating an optimal amalgam. But when we look at this combination to find reality around us, it leads us to another question. How do we know when someone tells us something genuinely and when there's something more beyond someone's initial statement? It's a vague way of wondering how to be a good judge of character.

Some people are very good at it, and for those of us who are still trying to master this trick, let's look at it in a little detail. We said there's a difference between letting a person start at the best level and assuming they're the best. When you meet a person, tell yourself you don't know anything about this person, positive or negative. There's also some truth in that we bring out certain aspects of the people around us. And each person is so unique that we cannot just label all people in certain categories. But to begin to understand human nature, concentrate on the subtle things, not the gross actions. It is easy to judge a person based on the large gestures they make, but many times that does not define a person. The subtle things give away a person's genuine character.

We said before that words are an imperfect way of communicating. We said so in reference to expressing our emotions and experiences, but it holds true here as well. Instead of focusing strictly on what a person says, look at their eyes. Think about it, why is eye contact so important in any social setting? Interviewers always look for strong eye contact and a firm handshake. When you're on a date, you always look for the other person to have their eyes on you, concentrating on what you have to say. So why is it that the eyes are such an important sense of ours, above all of the others? Because the eyes can never lie. There's always that unspoken understanding in them and maybe, if we studied it a bit further, we'd understand what they're trying to say.

Combine observation with experience and, like anything, we can learn over time. A lot of times when someone's speaking to you and they constantly divert their eye contact from you, you have to wonder why. Of course there are so many possibilities. Maybe the person is just shy or embarrassed. Maybe they're afraid what they say might hurt your feelings. Or maybe it's something a little more serious, like they're not being completely truthful with you, and they know it. But there's one thing in common in all of these situations: they are not comfortable. It may not necessarily be their fault or in their control, but if time and time again we notice the same habits in a person close to us, we mentally note that down and it's only natural to ask them what's going on. The eyes give us a gateway to knowing what's going on inside, and allow us to know this person better. Most of us don't think so consciously about all of this and hey, that's normal. But it's something to mull over and it's a solid way of working on a good judge of character.

Of course, most of us don't step out of our homes everyday and say, "Okay! Today I will be in control of everything around me! All conversations and interactions!" and it would be silly to say that, in any case. We can never control a situation completely, but at least we can be smart about not letting ourselves be taken advantage of. It's something to consider and at an age where we may assume we know everything, learning how to make the most of our relationships with others can apply to any setting, regardless of culture, location, and time. The best way to understand it is to try it out for yourself! Just observe and see people for who they really are, not who we want them to be.

I can't wait to get out of here.

It's a Friday evening in early May. Like all other weekend beginnings, you hung out with your three best friends during the afternoon and loved it. You four don't do anything spectacularly unique. Yet somehow, over years of binging on snacks and hot cocoa, a strong bond has been created. They just get you and you don't know how you'll survive without them.

Your mom calls your name and you snap back to reality. Family friends are coming for dinner in another half hour and the kitchen still needs to be cleaned up from your four-person powwow. It's always great having guests over and you love the atmosphere good company and food can bring. During dinner, the topic of your high school graduation comes up and it invites your stomach to run sets of somersaults. You smile, oblige the conversation, which is predominantly led by the adults at the table, finish your dinner quickly and excuse yourself. As you place your plate in the sink, you look out the window and see a summer evening setting into night with that beauty only your town can bring. You overhear the continued chatter from the dining room and quietly slip out onto the back porch.

You look up at the sky, take a deep breath, and take in that sweet summer aroma. And you reflect, like you have many an evening. As much as you love home, your family

*and friends, and where you grew up, you cannot wait to
burst out of small suburbia and see what else there is out
there in the world. You imagine traveling, meeting new
people, and everything else that's waiting for you outside
of home. Your new chapter begins in another three months
and you feel torn between the comfort of knowing home and
venturing outside to see what else is out there.*

*You notice dinner has finished inside and you store your
thoughts for another time and head back inside. As you slide
the glass door open, one last question comes into your mind,
"I love home, so why do I crave for something more?"*

Humans are creatures of curiosity. We like exploring
and learning more about the world around us. And
what's wrong in that? But isn't it nice to have a guideline
at times to know what others' experiences have been
with the same worldly concerns?

We previously identified different ways of analyzing
situations and although experience is one way, we do
not need to always start at zero to gain exposure to the
world around us. It takes a lot of time and, moreover, we
may not gain the experience we were hoping to get and

harm ourselves in the process. And that could be hard to recover from.

That being said, this world is seemingly limitless. So how could we not be excited to venture out and discover what it has to offer? If there were nothing to look forward to in life, our existence would be very boring, indeed. It's always good to live with something to look forward to, that way you never lose that desire to be active! But while embracing the fact that our world is vast, full of things positive and negative, we can't assume that what is outside of our homes is better than what is inside.

If we explore our surroundings completely, only then do we have the right to say we know what our entire environment has to give us and look for more.※ And isn't it easy to assume we know everything about our home, our family, and where we grew up? But the truth is, when we really think about it, what do we really know about, say, our parents? Sure, when we take off for college, we've known them for eighteen years. But what we know about them is how they are to us as parents; it's what we want to know about them, what we've taken for granted. But what were they like before they had us?

※   That could be in regard to any "environment". It just depends on how you define it.

What were their friends like growing up? Did they travel? What did they want to be when they grew up?≋ And the list goes on and on. So before we assume that the world outside home is better than what we grew up with, we must completely delve into what we have at home. And the best part is that our parents want to share these moments with us, too! They just don't know if we'd be interested. So we must make the effort to really "get to know" our parents. When we're older, wouldn't it be great to remember our parents by these memories and celebrate their lives?

But we can't just sit our parents down and abruptly ask, "Ok, tell me about your life." Patience fellow grasshoppers, we must wait for opportune instances. And who knows when that'll be? It could be on the drive to the grocery store, while watching TV, basically anytime and anywhere! And all it can take is one simple question. Like, you see a commercial with a dad teaching his kid how to ride a bike and you may wonder, did my grandparents teach my parents how to ride a bike? Ask

---

≋ My dad has told me many times about how much he wishes he had asked his parents more about their lives, their interests; anything to learn more about them than the fact that they were just his parents. Of course, at that time in India, you couldn't ask your parents much because it might not have been considered respectful. But I know he wishes he could have, and I do too, so that I could know more about my history.

that question! You might be surprised at the answer! Perhaps your grandparents did. Or perhaps your parents and all their friends saved up money together and bought a second-hand bike and took turns trying to ride it after school in the park. But you'll never know the answer unless you ask.

It's a blessing to have a culture and a heritage. We all have one and if we embrace it, we can share it with others, too. But if we reject our own background, we should not make the mistake of assuming that others will accept us better because of it. If we do not respect our roots, how can we expect others to? If we welcome our upbringing, others may be curious to learn more about it. To not take advantage of our heritage would be a personal loss.

So, when we think about it, neither "outside" nor "inside" is better than the other. There are positive aspects in both categories and we all live in limited environments. So how could we compare that to the world, which is seemingly infinite? We should respect the inside and find out as much as we can from it and be excited to know that we are never done learning about the outside. Life is so short and there's so much to see.

So long as we have that mentality, we will always be young.𖠰

And why do we need to do one before the other? Let us dive deeper at home while simultaneously exploring the outside. Why should we put a limit on what we make the most of in this life? Meet new people, see new places, try new things. Bring new dimensions to your life! And then come to a balance. Let's not assume we have all the answers at home, but use it as a guide and allow it to lead us to meet new experiences. Wouldn't it be nice if we could one day share these same thoughts with our future generations, years from now?

𖠰 Age has nothing to do with one's youth. We all have that one relative who's pushing eighty and still talks about what he or she wants to do when grown up. When you lose that feeling you become old, or worse yet, bland.

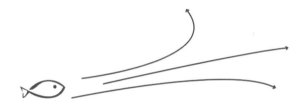

And the winner is...!

Your heart starts to skip beats here and there as you glance down intently at your college map. "Okay, Intro to Biology is in Kravitz Lecture Center...Kravitz, Kravitz, Kravitz...okay, found it. Now, how do I get there?" After circling around the lecture hall aimlessly for the ten minutes you allotted to your lack of navigation artistry, you come across the main entrance of the building. You walk through the two sets of double doors and find your assigned room immediately to your left and see dozens of students with confused faces matching yours streaming past you. You suddenly get an image of salmon jumping upstream in mass hordes.

Shaking the thought from your head, you put on your game face for your first college class. "Alright, this is going to be a piece of cake. You were in Honors Bio, AP Bio, the only student in your class to successfully remove the brains from a fetal pig and a cat. You got this." As you take in your classroom, you are shocked to see 470 seats more than what you were expecting. "Wait, this is an auditorium, not a classroom. Do I have the wrong place? Maybe this is for a theater class..." You quietly ask a student if this is Intro to Biology taught by Dr. Palmer and they confirm your schedule's instructions. And just in case you were planning on second-guessing that student, you see from across the hall a miniature version of your roommates waving you over to sit with them. As you walk in their direction, their figures gradually returning to their actual sizes, you think with relief that you have some familiar faces. You find your seat, get out your notebook, and look at the professor on stage and notice there's no chalkboard, not even a white board. There's a giant screen and a projector warming up. Oh, boy.

Your professor begins his lecture five minutes into the period and as you skim through the PowerPoint, you realize you're going to have to work a little harder than expected. But it should be no big deal. You were in your high school's National Honors Society. All that pre-collegiate preparation will definitely pay off here and you'll excel just like you did the past four years.

Before you know it, your first month at college has flown by and while walking out of your ninth Biology lecture, you and your roommates decide to study together for your exam that's two days away. You agree to meet back at the room at 6:00 this evening. You get pumped up for the upcoming study session and know you will rock it. You three all have the same science scholarship and you have a couple more friends from the program joining, so it'll amp up the competition that much more.

6:00 p.m. rolls around and as you and your friends gather round your common table, you notice you all have the *same eager look and confidence to begin. And so the drilling ensues. You take turns asking questions while the other four answer as fast as they can. To your surprise, your classmates are equally, if not more, quick to answer the questions. You assume you are just rusty, but by the end of the two-hour bout, you are left feeling confused. Not about the material for the test, but about the rate at which your classmates were able to tackle the questions. You begin to doubt yourself and your success in high school. "Am I really as smart as I thought I was? Maybe my success in high school wasn't as great as I thought. I assumed if I got all the accolades I did in school, that I'd be the top of my class in further studies too." As you put away your notes and book you start to doubt your past accomplishments and wonder: what was the point?*

From the time we were young, we've been told life is goal-driven. Everything we want to be can only be accomplished by achieving certain things. If you reach these goals, you are a success. If not, you are a failure. But are things in life really this black and white? What if the goals in life are a moving target, not just a stationary stepping stone to this elusive concept we've coined, called success?

Compared to the conventional thought of a stationary goal, a moving target is unsettling. The story at the beginning of this chapter is a common situation many of us have experienced in some context. But if we look at our specific example, how many of us believed after our high school graduation, that if we had taken all our AP classes, joined any and all extracurricular activities, and were involved with as many Honors societies as possible, we would reach success? Even if we did check off all of these things on our success list, then what? We've proven we're smart. But when we reach college, there comes that inevitable realization that there are many people who have obtained the same things we have. We did what we were supposed to do, so why aren't we standing out amongst those around us? Isn't that what success is?

But "success" is such a subjective term. And a moving target is a much harder concept to wrap your head around. In essence, it seems like an oxymoron: how can you ever reach a moving target? But that's just it; maybe it's not about that final outcome that we assume is success. Maybe it's about the trek we take to get there. How do we know there's ever a final outcome, anyway?

There's never an end to anything in life, be it knowledge, education, or money.

Think about it: when are you ever considered rich? Isn't that all in relation to what you're comparing it to? The definition of rich is when you have a little more than what you previously had. So just when you think you've accomplished that goal of gaining a certain amount of wealth, you're told that you haven't. So then, at what stage can you say you're rich? If you have $100,000 that's a lot more than what a person with $10,000 has. So you can safely assume, *Yes, I am rich.* But what if you come across someone else who has a million dollars? What are you now?

If we look at life at such a small scale, frustration will always be a peripheral outcome on our way to success. Thankfully, the solution seems to be quite simple. Instead of looking at a single target, why don't we look at the incremental change from yesterday to today? Let's look at "where I was" as opposed to "where I want to be." That's not to say we should not be ambitious. But must we define success as something that's always right in front of us?

Alright, so what? Now we're supposed to constantly look behind us? No! If we think we've reached all we can already, how can we ever be inspired to strive for more? Instead, if we split our satisfaction into two aspects, perhaps we can finally reach a solution to this predicament. Let us be satisfied with what we have at this point in time, but not be satisfied with status quo. Another oxymoron? No, it's really not. It's all about being on that path towards your destination. There will never be any brick wall that prevents us from moving forward, unless we put it there ourselves. If we realize there's never an end to growing and it's a cycle, we'll constantly be able to increase in strength. We're born knowing something and we die not knowing everything. From the moment we arrive at the hospital nursery, we know who our mother is, we know how to ask for food, attention, a clean diaper, even. When we die, we definitely accept the fact that we don't know everything there is to know.

This realization, that there is no beginning and no end, is the biggest understanding we can come to. We have the capacity and the potential to grow every day, even if it is just a little bit. That incremental change is the true success in life. If we assume that to be smart, rich, or happy, we need to reach a certain point, we will never reach it, because it will always be just a step ahead of us. If only it were that easy; that we could merely set a goal, reach it, and be satisfied. But once we reach it, we always want a little bit more, to go a little bit further. Why should we be miserable for no reason? Let's stop thinking there is a finite target in anything, because there isn't. Therein lies the key to happiness. The days we are sad are the days there are no incremental changes from the day before. And maybe that's the reason why many people give up. They've tried for so long and keep trying to reach a finite point of success and just can't do it any more. They settle for that escapism and sit on the sidelines.

And for those who claim they already know everything, that claim is merely a false security. Deep down, we know no one has the answers to everything, but some would like to convince themselves that they do, that they've reached that big, final target. That's such an easy way to stop moving and to say that you've already reached an end. There's that self-planted brick wall! Those who say they already know everything have an insecure side to them, that's probably just beneath the surface. They know they don't know everything, and yet it's hard to accept that fact.

So let us not cry and lament over things in the past. No one is perfect, and that's the key point in this chapter. The question is not whether you will reach perfection, because none of us ever will. We should actually be asking ourselves, are we headed towards perfection? If that's your goal and that is your direction, you've already reached your destination because nobody is perfect. There is no end to end all, and to assume so would cause a lot of wear and tear on the system. Why shouldn't we enjoy the accomplishments we have thus far? It's a much better route than to crib about what we don't have. And if we think we'd be happy if we had those specific things we don't have, we wouldn't. Instead, let's ask ourselves if we are headed in the right direction. If we escape, think: there is nothing to be afraid of, nothing to be insecure about, and there is no ultimate goal except the journey.[≋] While we work our way to keeping on the right path, let us celebrate others' success in doing the same. Let's enjoy our previous motion and keep moving.

As long as we keep chugging along, we will continuously be successful. Along the way, it's only natural that the things we do on our path will change. We will not be doing the same things we do in our 20s in our 30s, 40s, and 50s. But we'll travel to where we're

---

≋   If this were a musical, we'd definitely break into song right about now.

supposed to go. Not only will we go in the right direction and grow, but we'll always be happy. And when we're happy, it shows. Who wants to be around someone who is constantly bitter or upset that they haven't reached a certain point in their life? People don't buy a smile attempting to mask disappointment. But we'll never be dissatisfied if we keep pushing forward. It's a simple concept and doesn't require much research. But many accomplished people never realize this. If we recognize this notion, we'll encourage our desire to constantly strive for more and not stop where we are.

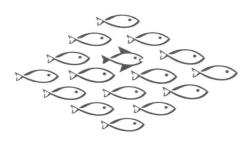

Two peas.

That's it; that's all you can endure of engineering. You gave it your best shot. You gave your all in every class, for every semester, but you never found that "click" you assumed you would in any of your courses over the past two years. There has to be another major that intrigues you the way you had expected engineering would. As you walk out of your school's main dining hall, feeling frustrated and disappointed, you see an informational for incoming engineering majors to be held this evening. Seniors in various fields of engineering will host the event. Taking this observation as a sign from above, you think to yourself: 'Ok, this is my last attempt. I don't want to have to go into another major. I hope these people have the answers to my worries. They're seniors; I'm sure some of them have gone through a problem like mine.'

You look forward to the informational with ridiculously high levels of hope and a few hours later find yourself seated in the first row of a small and intimate room. You're on time and are the only one there sans the five seniors in the front of the room. After a few minutes, underclassmen trickle in and the informational finally begins. You listen to the speeches of the hosts and your ears perk up when one of the students mentions his difficulty settling into the mechanical engineering department and how, at times, he finds himself reconsidering his major.

After the introductions conclude, the seniors offer an
open forum for the guests to ask any questions they may
have about engineering. You immediately make a beeline
over to the doubtful engineer and strike up a conversation
with him. You pour your heart out to him and wait hopefully
for his response to your engineering sob story. Finally, you'll
know what to do with your undergraduate career; whether
switching majors is a good idea, if you should take a lighter
load of classes, if it's best to stick it out in engineering. After
a pause, your hopeful Yoda begins a long monologue about
how he knows how you feel and how hard engineering
classes are. But to your dismay, after hanging on to his every
word, you realize that it's just a bunch of jargon and your
questions are not quite answered.

"So would taking a lighter load be a good idea?"

"It might but it'll only take you longer to get out of here."

"Ok. Well, how are the job opportunities for a Bachelor's
in engineering?"

"With the economy the way it is, it's gonna be hard to get
a job with any degree."

"Are you happy you stayed in engineering?"

"Well, it's better trying to stick it out than to start from
scratch in another subject." he ends with a chuckle.

After your conversation you thank him for his time and speak to the other seniors for a few minutes. You get some good ideas for scheduling classes for future semesters and leave with a meditative feeling in your gut. As you walk back to your dorm room, you reflect on the opinion of the doubtful engineer. "Is it really better to stick it out if I just don't like engineering? What if I end up disliking my job after graduation, too? Is it really worth it? I thought talking to a student who had similar concerns as mine would solve my problems, but now I just feel that much more confused."

A couple of hours later, as you crawl into bed and close your eyes, they immediately snap back open as you remember with dread that you have another problem set due tomorrow afternoon in your circuits class. Choosing procrastination as your guiding light, you close your eyes again and roll over to face the wall. You've reached a super-saturated level of engineering contemplation for one day.

More times than not, it holds true that unasked for advice is rarely listened to and absorbed. And it's a common phenomenon for elders to feel obligated to give you advice, be it good, bad, valuable, or not. We've all had that experience of tuning someone out. We may not make our indifference externally apparent, but the solicitude of others is wasted on us in these moments.

Sound advice is not necessarily an issue of age, though; it's general human nature. If someone tells you they've noticed you've been exhibiting a certain behavior and they've learned through experience that that behavior only leads to bad outcomes, you might just listen and take their opinion for what it's worth. But if someone constantly tells you what you're doing is wrong, you will eventually tune him or her out. It's only natural to ask (outwardly or inwardly), "Who asked you?"

And if you go out of your way to ask someone for guidance, you would only approach someone if you thought that person had expert knowledge in that topic. You wouldn't go to your English teacher for help in calculus, right? There's a glitch in this thought process, though. Looking at it on a broader scale, we assume that older people, having gone through more stages of life than us, would have the experience that would give them wisdom. But that may not hold true. Perhaps this person may not have had the experiences you think they should have had by now. Be it a matter of career, education, personal life, some people may have more experience in one area and much less in others, with no regard to what their age is. With no intention of undermining these people, they might have just lived very protected lives.

Or maybe it's that experience, when you think about it, does not just pop into existence merely because someone is subjected to a situation. If comes from understanding the context of the situation, understanding what happened, and learning some lessons from it. That is, it's the difference between simple exposure to events and actual experience. Events occur outside us, but experience develops from within. We need to observe, contemplate, draw some conclusions, and store those conclusions for future use before we can say we have experience in a given subject. Lots of times, people dishing out advice haven't done all of this.

It's not about a generation gap between old and young, that somehow older people always have the answers; it's about having expertise in a certain domain. If you have consultants for finance in a company, you're paying them for their advice. If, after some time, you notice they don't have ideas any better than yours, why would you keep them around for help? You can guide yourself equally, if not better, than them. Just because someone appears to have the credentials, doesn't mean they have the experience and knowledge you had assumed. Alright, so that being said, why do we always assume that people with whom we share common exposure to certain events will understand us and we will, in the process, find comfort in camaraderie? Are we really two peas in a pod? Maybe the reason we tend to listen to them is because there is some common event we share with them and when we try to explain our concern with the situation, the other person seems to understand completely. Perhaps, deep down, we know that we're not talking to them for guidance; we're not assuming they have the answer. But at least we have the comfort of knowing others seem to understand our problem. And when they give us their conclusion on the topic, it could be right for them but wrong for us. Just because we may share similar problems with our confidant doesn't mean that the conclusion the other person drew would be the same that we would come to. A person's conclusion depends on that person's nature and background. It would be misleading to think that because there is a shared problem experience, it will result in a shared answer experience. Of course, that could happen if the other person is very similar to you in thought processes and background. But how often does that occur? Enough for us to rely on it on a uniform basis? Probably not. And maybe what we would get out of this experience is very different from what the other person got out of it.

When we look at the story for this chapter, it seems like we chose a pseudo-Yoda. In reality, the senior soon to graduate from college in engineering did not have any sound advice. What he chose for himself may be what he thought was best for him. And it definitely is not what's best for us. If our distaste for engineering is strong now, why should we assume we have to put up with it for the rest of our lives? Engineering is great for those who find their "click" in trusses and circuits. But if it's not for us, that's ok! Why should we assume what others have chosen for themselves is what's best for us? It's not a mistake to get off the so-called beaten path and try something else. Maybe we'll find our "click" in another major. And maybe we'll even graduate on time. We know what it'll be like if we stick with engineering (or whatever our current problem is), but we don't know what would happen if we take a different route. And even if this new path doesn't click with us, it's ok! At least we tried, and that can prove to be fortuitous, even if it doesn't seem so immediately.

Sometimes taking a chance is a blessing in disguise. Let us not put ourselves down completely. We've talked about how we're the ones who know us best. We've also talked about listening to that reliable gut of ours whose opinion usually proves to be beneficial. Listen to others; those deep thinkers. Absorb their takes on situations, and then mull over all of that and make the call for yourself. Even if others' conclusions don't gel with us, we can learn from their thoughts and mold our own. If we look to others to sketch out our plans entirely, how can we ever be wise enough to help others if they come to us for advice, some time down the road?

YOLO, Dr. Huxtable.

As you feel yourself float to the surface from the depths of deep sleep, you refuse to open your eyes. But you feel the sensation of someone shining a flashlight directly onto your eyelids. Your eyelids flap back like window blinds and you sigh as you see the sun has risen before you, once again. You grab your phone and stare at its screen with one eye (you might as well give the other one a break). It's 6:17 on a typical autumn morning. You think with frustration and longing of those extra thirteen minutes intended for sleep and drag yourself out of bed.

Entering your bathroom, you grab your toothbrush and commence your morning routine. As you begin to brush your teeth you look around your bedroom. It's a funny feeling coming home and not having an itinerary to leave in nine days at the end of your Spring Break. This is your home now; again. But this time, coming home feels different. You enjoy being home, but you always assumed you'd be out living on your own in an exciting big city with a flashy job immediately after graduation.

Forty-five minutes later you dash out of the house, coffee thermos in hand, and messenger bag strapped across you. You climb into your car and slam the car door shut, simultaneously shoving the car key into the ignition. As you head down the same route you always take for work, you *think of your friends from college. You miss them terribly and think of all the fun memories you made with them over four years. In a way, you became more than just friends; there was a shade of kinship created and it feels unnatural to be so far from them. How easy it was to just pick up the phone and text one of them to meet up for a walk, a club meeting, or a midnight snack! And it only took five minutes to reach them, as opposed to the miles that separate you from them now.*

You remember how many times you all said you couldn't wait to graduate, go back home, and start another chapter. And here you are, driving to your job, making money, and finally living in the comfort of your own home, back in your hometown. Is the grass really always greener away from where we are at present? Finally, you have the life you worked so hard for during those four years and you're in that transitioning stage from post grad to real life workaholic. You've gone from late night study sessions, hopped up on energy drinks, to nine-to-five work schedules. But aren't you on the track to where you want to eventually be? Wasn't the final goal to be working, settled, and content?

You turn on the radio and fiddle with the stations until you come across a song from a couple of years ago that you and your friends used to dance to in your dorm room. A smile crosses your face and you listen, possibly for the first time, to the lyrics. "Party" is repeated about ten times to the beat of a strong bass and, if paraphrased, the message is to enjoy staying out late, stop thinking and planning for the future, and forget about what happens tomorrow; live like you've only got today.

You suddenly view this song from a different perspective. You've heard these generic opinions in all the radio singles. If they're all saying the same thing, maybe there's some truth to what they say. You listen to the words again. There's no way you want to stay up late anymore; you're exhausted by 7:00 p.m.! Your friends from home are the same: working and saving money for the future. You know you're not alone in your grandma status. But where is that carefree nature the artist is talking about? You wonder, "Do I not have that anymore? Did I ever have that? Did I pass by the most exciting time of my life and not even know it?"

Each of us has our own set of goals and expectations for the future. But society has a lot to say and a lot of influence on how our goals can be morphed along the way to achieving them. Sometimes, society can have good points and give our ideas some perspective. But many more times, we feel a certain pressure, often at a subconscious level, that what we are doing is not what society would agree to be success.

If you think about it, whether it's from mainstream musicians, actors, or any public figure, they all have a message in common: instant gratification. It's not a new concept; it's been said in different ways over time. And the basis of it is made up of three factors. The first is intoxication of some kind. I don't mean getting smashed necessarily. Rather, without sounding too much like a textbook, intoxication can be more broadly defined as fascination with a thrilling sensation. The second is flirting with danger, or dangerous consequences. And the third is not actually accepting the truth of reality. Add these three up and you've got the supposed recipe for immediate perks. We need to question, why are people telling us this works? Whether it's a song, a show, a movie, or a magazine, it's a marketing scheme and it's a way to make money.

Are there any other options? People can either sell you the idea of instant gratification, or they could tell you that's it's not the right way to lead your life; that you should always think of life in the long run. Gone are the days of Dr. Huxtable speaking humorous worldly truths to his children. The first message makes a lot more money and is much easier to sell. If the second group wanted to make money from their message, they'd have to wait a long time to prove their theory is worthwhile. The former's success is also instant gratification in a way.

So when we listen to a message of instant gratification, it's subliminally disconcerting. It goes against what we were taught for years in school, or even at home. That we have to work for what we want, that all things come in due time. You may think of times when you tried the route of instant gratification and it blew up in your face. But then you recall what you had heard on the radio, in a movie, a talk show, wherever. *"This famous person is telling me it's ok to live merely for instant gratification. And if millions of people are listening to this message, then it has to be right. Maybe there's something wrong with me, if I don't agree completely with it".* But maybe everybody has that same thought as you. Maybe no one is truly convinced that this is the best route.

But there are aspects of society that put a brake on this message for many people. For some, it's the general disapproval of others. For others, familial pressure can

play a huge role in one's behavior. If you know your
parents, siblings, and grandparents would disapprove of
your behavior, it will probably limit the extent to which
you live without any concerns. And if you continue to
do something you know deep down would make them
cringe, you will do everything in your power to keep
them from finding out. Religion is another social brake.
It gives people security in knowing that a collective
group can give them strength. One may not want to
sacrifice all of that for instant gratification.

Of course, no one thinks consciously about all of
this, but perhaps this is what happens at a deeper level.
Something has to push back against the advertisement of
instant gratification. But if you don't have any pressure
coming from any direction, you will give in totally to
this marketing. And the selfish side of us wants to have
our cake and eat it too. People want to have morals, but
they also want to have instant pleasure. It's possible we
assume we can push our morals and responsibilities for
later; focus on them in the long run, in broad and vague
spectrums. But if we live with that in mind, we'll never
really practice those virtues.

And why do we fear there is some small time window,
where all of our actions have no repercussions, and it's

slipping from our grasp? Is there an assumption that at some point we are losing our freedom? Why does the media tell us that we are losing our freedom if we get married, if we have children, if we grow up? The reality is that we're never actually completely free, unless we renounce ourselves from society altogether.

But if we define freedom from a slightly different view, we can definitely state we are free. We are always free to think whatever we like, good or bad. Nobody can stop you from thinking, from being at peace with yourself, from aspiring to be whatever you want to be. On the other hand, nobody can stop you from thinking bad thoughts, either. The perceived thoughts of another's attitude are just what we see from the outside. We only see that person's behavior and the action that comes from it. But inside, they are free. Similarly, we will never give that freedom up, no matter what; even if we get married, have children, and settle down.

Ok, what if you have no plans of marriage or children? You're still never completely free. So long as we live in a society, we are never truly "free". And that's alright; we have that obligation to society. If we claim we are free, why do we call another for comfort when we're upset, why do we call our parents for money? If people are supporting us, how can we claim that we are free to do whatever we want without keeping their concerns in mind as well? Our actions will have an effect on the people around us and vice versa. So let's live according to the greater good. If we want to live in a society (be it a nation, family, or a group of friends) and we reject all their work towards a communal good, we will eventually be rejected. And once rejected, it's so hard to get back into that group.

So if we agree that we are never truly free, then what is it that people are afraid of losing? Perhaps it's not really freedom we're worried about. Maybe it's the thought of gaining responsibilities. Whether we're talking about marriage, parenthood, or jobs, it's just laziness. That feeling of just wanting to "have fun" and get by is a disguise for shirking responsibilities. Hopefully, there are people who care about us enough to tell us that's not the most beneficial way to live. Even if we're only concerned about our own wellbeing, the best way to help ourselves is to help others, right? When we do that, we become a better person as a whole and society celebrates us for that. If we take this as our message, then we will grow to see that it's senseless to think that we can take whatever we want for ourselves with no concern for others. If we all did that, then everyone would suffer from each other's actions.

Think about it this way: take a group of five people. If each person only looks out for himself or herself, each person has just one person caring for him or her. But if each person didn't look after himself or herself at all and, instead, focused on caring for the other four people, then each person would have four people looking after him or her. The pleasure is never in taking; it's always in giving. And unless we experience that for ourselves, we'll never understand how beautiful that phrase is. When we take, we enjoy for a moment. But when we give, we get a happiness that lasts much longer.

So what do we want? If we truly want happiness, let us use our energy to help others. And why can't this be fun too? Why can't we have fun thinking and working for our future? Why can't we have fun and enjoy helping others as much as if we were directly helping only ourselves? It's guaranteed to bring you happiness. If we only give in to our base instincts for satisfaction, we're not living life to the fullest or using ourselves to our full capacity. Let us dream about our future; after all, it's a part of living life in the present.

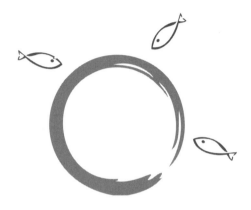

Lean on me.

At 7:30 p.m., *you throw your bag on the floor with a sigh. You are always surprised at how heavy your laptop feels when bolstered against your back. You collapse on to your sofa and grab your phone. Looking at the date at the top of the screen, you notice tomorrow marks the start of November. Already? It feels like summer was just a few weeks ago. Your weekly schedule has led you to view the majority of this year in a flash. You made a timeline in June to outline all the things you wanted to accomplish for yourself. And over the months, its constant evolution has permitted you continuous extensions for all your deadlines.*

You drop your phone on the ground and lie on your back. Stretching your legs straight with a giant yawn, you lift your arms until your elbows lock and your hands are in line with your face. You stare at your separated fingers and then past them to the ceiling, a habit you had formed in your childhood, dedicated to when you take time to ponder.

You think of your high school years and the targets you had set for yourself, your college years when those targets altered and evolved sometimes into goals completely different, and finally to the present where you find yourself reflecting fondly on the past and looking into the future with anticipation. Thinking again of your timeline, you question how you will finish all your desires for this year. If you have all these demands lined up for yourself, how will you ever be able to set aside any time to do more for others, like you always claim you will? Don't we have to help ourselves before we can help others?

Hearing the jingling of keys outside the garage door, you snap out of your trance and sit up in time to see your mom come through the door, back from another hard day at work. You get up and catch up with her as you make her a cup of tea. As you listen to how her day went, you mindlessly take out your timeline from your bag, slash out the written deadlines, and write in another batch of two-week extensions.

W hy do we classify living for ourselves and living for some "greater purpose" as two different things? Maybe if we make ourselves the greater purpose, we'd be able to come to a compromise. Why must we declare that we can only have one or the other; that we can either have fun or we can suffer for the sake of others?

At the end of the day, all of us want something for ourselves. The fact that we're asking these questions in the first place means that we want some personal good. When we want something good, and that "greater purpose" is ourselves, it leads us to another question: what do we want for ourselves? But that really depends on how short-lived our planning for the future is. We usually want things because we think it'll give us happiness and excitement in life. If we buy a new car it's a great thrill, but that new car will become old as soon as another model comes out and we'll lose that momentary delight.

Then how do we decide on an appropriate duration for our future plans? If we split duration into three categories, based on what the duration could give us, we'd have the following. An extremely short duration could be as long as it takes to eat an ice cream. That can give us a fleeting pleasure but if we want a sense of excitement and a sense of fulfillment, that only can come from accomplishments.

This is our second duration. Define an accomplishment for yourself; don't allow society to do that work for you.⁂ Take this upon yourself. And be

---

⁂ Society perceives and defines things with generic and uniform ideals in mind. On a daily basis, our minds are pounded with information on what defines a person as beautiful; that it is something to work for and is an accomplishment if one achieves it. But that varies from country to country. A tanned complexion is highly coveted in North American culture but in Asia, the fairer you are, the more beautiful you are. I'll take my "wheat-ish complexion", thank you very much.

ambitious! Set goals slightly beyond what you can do. The thrill of knowing you may fail is what gives you the drive to seek for more. Sometimes, you will fail, but when you achieve your goal, it will be something to truly relish. If there is a chance of failure, we should know how to accept and overcome it. Anytime we do something that has a risk factor (we're not talking about risky business, here), there is a possibility of not reaching your target. We can't expect to win every time. You know the risks you are taking are high enough when you fail at times. And sometimes, the reason you fail could be due to external components. So when we are met with failure, how do we deal with it?

The third duration could be everlasting if it has one key ingredient: bliss. Well that sounds well and good if it were so easy to have. And maybe it is. Where can we find bliss? The only place it's found is in knowledge. Let's say we put our level of happiness on a spectrum, where depression is "−infinity" and bliss is "+infinity". When you try to be happy and it doesn't happen, you will obviously feel worse. But if your starting value is above zero, even if you fall a little, you will not feel completely sad.

We need to be blissful. But what is bliss, exactly? Simply said, it's the ability to feel good even when things are going in a negative direction. Kind of sounds like a super power. But it's not impossible to possess. If we have knowledge that life is more than what's right in front of us, anything (good or bad) can happen on the outside and we'll be good to go on the inside.♒ And merely accomplishing things does not make everyone content. People who have accomplished many things by society's standards are still not happy.

If we keep, on average, a high level of contentedness, we'll find that the little things will not bother us. Perhaps we can make this our own communal goal. We know there's the chance of failure, but if we work at it, we can reach bliss. To do so, we'll need to understand two things. The first is to understand how the universe functions. I don't mean this in a cosmic sense, just that we need to understand the world around us. And second, we need to understand how human nature functions. Bliss is a harmony between the two.

Take a large body of water, like the Atlantic Ocean. We cannot disturb it easily. Even if we catapult a

---

♒ On the flipside, if you eat an ice cream for momentary enjoyment, if you are already below zero on our happiness scale, having an ice cream may make you feel better but it will not necessarily make you feel good.

mammoth boulder into it, it may create some ripples, but it will definitely not muddle the entire body into frenzy. Knowledge is just like that. Even when things come your way that could cause negativity, it will not shake you. It gives you perspective of what's happening around you. And when you see that interaction between external and internal environments, it confirms what you know and inspires you to learn more.

In a way, to find bliss, we need detached attachment. I know what you're thinking: another oxymoron? But if we contemplate on the term a little more, we'll see that it's not actually a contradictory statement. Be attached to the effort but detached from the outcome. When we have a level of knowledge that gives us this state of Zen, we can finally experience bliss.

And the best thing about bliss is that it's eternal. So long as we're aware of it, we'll always have it. How great would it be to reach this level of stability? If we make ourselves the greater purpose, we'll be able to help ourselves and, in turn, help those around us. We all need that person who's our rock; the person we can always lean on. How awesome would it be if we could be that rock for those around us? Maybe that, in itself, is the enjoyment, the accomplishment, and the bliss we're all looking for.

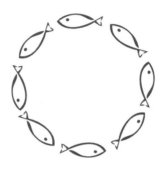

Circle of Life.

W*alking through the gates of your hometown park, you find a familiar bench showing its skin through a cracking coat of green paint. You sit down and face yourself in the direction of the swing set and look around the field. You loved this park for being adjacent to your childhood neighbourhood and, now, love it even more for not changing a bit.*

As you take in the sun's warmth, like a cozy blanket on this early spring afternoon, you feel goose bumps on your bare legs and think of all the times, like today, that you've taken your summer shorts out a little too early. You throw your head back, appreciating the perfectly blue sky and the few cotton-ball clouds and close your eyes. You hear children laughing and smile to yourself. The familiar recap of your childhood, adolescence, and adult years plays in your head like an old home video reel. You think of many moments; when you thought life was at its best hour, when you thought things couldn't get any worse, lessons learned, and you chuckle to yourself sitting here on this reliable, old bench and come to the conclusion that there's so much to be grateful for; even the small things, like this flawless, lazy day.

Just as you are about to feel the friendly embrace of an afternoon nap, a small hand tugs at your left pointer finger. You open your eyes at look down at a small child.

"Whatcha doing?" the child asks with those giant, curious dark eyes. You notice the same long eyelashes as your sister's and you smile.

"Just thinking," you answer.

"'Bout what?"

You pick up your fun-sized nephew, place him on your lap, and try to come up with an answer.

When we look back on our life (no matter how old or young we are), there's a certain similarity we share of looking at times both good and bad. Sometimes we reflect on our own, and other times it may be triggered by something we see at present day, an event that takes us back to a particular moment from which we've taken away something. Call it a lesson or a note to one's self, we've all had that commonality.

But there are also many times when we've assumed we've learned a lesson only to come to realize that we never did; that days, months, years down the road, we continue to make the same mistakes. So how do we recognize a mistake and learn from it?

Perhaps the best way to start is to really wonder, *"what is a mistake?"* Is it merely having your preconceived notion proven wrong or is it something more? If it were just to have our assumption proven wrong, then why do we make the same mistake more than once? We need more than just our conjectures denied validity. We need to take away an experience from that mistake.

If we are honest about a mistake we have made, we need to own up to it. Forget about the people around us in this matter; we need to own up to ourselves. To shrug off the responsibility of accepting you made a mistake would only be a lie to yourself. It's alright to make a mistake; we all have made mistakes and we'll continue to make mistakes. But if we can at least learn from mistakes we have made in the past by walking away with an experience, we can make progress in our personal growth, instead of simply adding to our list of unresolved blunders. If we continue to make the same errors over and over again, it's really just a waste of our time. And that is a mistake we need to learn from.

To think things happen to us without our involvement is not accurate. And going off that note, if we take a stand that things in the universe must always behave in a way suitable to us, it'll never work because it'll never happen. If we know a certain situation will have an inimical outcome for us, we need to remove ourselves from that situation. I know you love my oversimplified examples (but really, they can be applied to many scenarios) so here comes another! Let's say you are starting your fourth week at your first job and you want to be that new addition to the company, beloved by all your co-workers. But there's that one guy who is so annoying; to the point where you can't think of anything else except how much he irritates you. You call your friend on your drives back home from work to vent out your frustration, but it only leaves you feeling crappy with guilt, knowing your colleague is not that bad a guy, he's just super annoying.

Take a step back from this situation and think. Why is this colleague so annoying? For one thing, he can't be irritating if we don't allow ourselves to be irritable. Since he works in the same area as us, we can't completely avoid him; and we don't need to. What we do need to avoid is the annoyance we associate with him. If that means not having extended conversations with him, that's alright. It's better to be calm and reliable at work, as opposed to being the person that talks about another co-worker with disdain. For all you know, months down the road, you two may become better acquainted and become friends. Why throw that option away by continuing to be petty? We can't alter those around us, but we can change how we react to others and the (positive or negative!) effect they have on us.

If we try to view things in this manner, each way we make a mistake, we'll learn to avoid it in the future. Like I said before, I realize that a situation may come our way many times, and the outcomes may be different each time. But when we allow ourselves to get deeply involved emotionally in a certain circumstance, it is that much harder for us to accept that we made a mistake and that we need to overcome it. To the best extent possible, if we reduce the level to which we become emotionally involved, we will not fall for the mistake in the future.

At present day and in the future, it's safe to say we'd all like to lead our lives in a way such that others can learn. Don't we all want to be those rocks of strength for others, especially for future generations? Apart from just being human hot cocoas of comfort, how can we help others learn from their mistakes as well? If we just tell

---

≋ We can't help others if they don't want to be helped. Many times people who come to you with a problem may just be looking for confirmation in their own set beliefs. But if someone younger comes to us for guidance, shouldn't we be prepared sufficiently to mentor him or her wisely?

them our own personal experiences, it may not mean anything to them. The conversation has to be catered to the audience in such a way that its content is relatable and resonates beyond just the heart-to-heart. If we give examples in that context, it is more likely that the connection between the cause and effect of a situation will surface and the person asking for help will take away something valuable from the conversation.

For any of us to learn from others, we need to listen, contemplate, and apply what we've been presented with. That way, we can learn and create our own experiences, thereby gaining our own take on the matter. We can't learn if we don't seek. And sometimes the beginning of that journey lies with us making some mistakes along the way.[≈] There's no need to stress on our mistakes. Instead, we can focus on what we've learned from them and charge forward with that new nugget of encouragement for the future.

≈   There is a quote by Katrin Green that says, "My one advice: focus on what you have— not what you've lost." Although I'm pretty sure she was referring to hurdles and meter dashes, her statement made me realize that it's not just me who has felt they've made mistakes in their life. And the world is not going to end because of our mistakes. We should be thankful for what we have and strive for more.

Leaving so soon?

Before we flip to the back cover, let me leave you with this last thought...

Why turn over a new leaf when you can turn to a whole new book? That's exactly what I've done. I've learnt a lot about myself, who I thought I was, who I thought I wanted to be. I've learnt quite a bit about the world around me and what all it can offer. I suppose my greatest lesson learnt was that I'm not done learning; nowhere near done. And maybe I'll never be done. And that's okay with me because that means I'll always have more room to grow.

So here's to life and the ridiculous variety of lemons it throws at us. Here's to a new book. Here's to the future and the wonderful anticipation of wondering what's next.

From the bottom of my heart …

I'd like to take this moment to thank a few important people, without whom this book definitely would not exist. First, I would like to thank my parents, P. R. and Vanditha Mukund, for everything they have given me. I'm more than fortunate to know you both.

Next, I would like to thank Katherine Kendig for giving me the best feedback and encouragement I could ask for while editing this book's manuscript. Thank you to all my friends for the awesome memories that inspired many of my stories. A big thank you to the team at Resource Design who worked many hours to ensure this book's design is perfect.

And finally, I'd like to thank you, the reader, for giving me a bit of your time to share my thoughts with you.